The 50s & 60s Kitchen

A Collector's Handbook & Price Guide

Jan Lindenberger

Schiffer Publishing Ltd

77 Lower Valley Road, Atglen, PA 19310

Magnetic bottle openers. Wooden figures
with metal guitars. $40-60 each.

Copyright © 1994 by Jan Lindenberger
Library of Congress Catalog Number:
93-87048

Printed in the United States of America
ISBN: 0-88740-591-6

We are interested in hearing from authors
with book ideas on related topics.

DESIGNED BY MARK S. BALBACH

Title page photo: Plastic fruit people wired
together and sequined eyes. $12-15 for the
pair.

Opposite page: Ceramic egg plate trimmed in
gold. California Originals. 10". $15-18.

Published by Schiffer Publishing Ltd.
77 Lower Valley Road
Atglen, PA 19310
Please write for a free catalog.
This book may be purchased from the publisher.
Please include $2.95 postage.
Try your bookstore first.

Acknowledgements

I wish to give a special thank you to John and Chris at Firefly Antiques in Manitou Springs, Colorado for opening up their shop and home to allow me to photograph, and for giving me much of the valuable information for this book.

Special thanks to Beth Hillgren for all her help and participation in this endeavor.

Also thanks to the following people and anyone whom I may have forgotten:

Anne's Antiques, Colorado Springs, Colorado
Antique Gallery, Littleton, Colorado
Antique Mall of Lakewood, Lakewood, Colorado
Atomic, Denver, Colorado
Burlington Arcade Mall, Lincoln, Nebraska
Central Park Antique Mall, Bakersfield, California
Darlene's, Kansas City, Missouri
Joe and Patsy Sadler, Bakersfield, California
Judy Walton, Longmont, Colorado
Maine Street Antique Mall, Ozark, Missouri
Mario Rivoli, Denver, Colorado
Myke Johnson, Denver, Colorado
Random Pickin's, Longmont, Colorado
Tojo's, Chowchilla, California
Washburn View Antique Mall, Topeka, Kansas
Wheatland Antique Mall, Topeka, Kansas

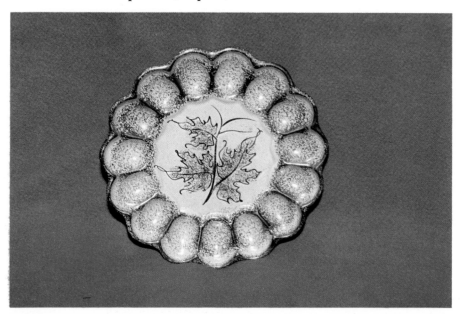

Plastic padded chair and wrought iron base.
$35-45.

Contents

Introduction

Whether you lived through the 1950s and 1960s, or have just gained a love for the era by looking back at it, it is unlikely that you will experience a period quite like it every again. For you collectors of the wonderful 50s-60s kitchen collectibles, I hope this book will help you better understand the why's and wherefore's of this period. Whoever thought it up, they created a wild time. Beware! You are in for a lot of fun.

Among the products of the 50s and 60s were the Sputnik, fall out shelters, and the threat of nuclear annihilation. As odd as it may seem, the cold war had a strong influence in our kitchen. You see, the companies that were major defense contractors also made kitchen appliances. They took that button that everyone feared, put it into kitchen appliances (push buttons). They inferred that these appliances were complex, competent, powerful, and would release you from household drudgery. With the new technology came the coining of the phrase "household convenience".

During the post war period of the early 50s the United States manufacturers probably produced more, and the consumer used more, than we will ever again. The rapid changes in science and technology led to the underlying belief that things weren't supposed to last. There was always something better just around the corner. Hence planned and built in obsolescence. This was a dramatic shift from the scarcity people experienced during the Depression and the war years.

Lots of dramatic changes were taking place. People were moving out of the cities and away from the extended family situation into a place called a "suburb." The homes that people bought in the suburbs were split level, open and airy. Plus, they came with a new thing! Built-ins.

For the first time people began to commute long distances to work. The role of women gradually went from homemaker to working mother. All of this left less time for that closeness and family feeling that they had left. To fill this void there was the rise of the back yard barbecue, cocktail parties and picnics. To release the tension of all this "fun" we consumed a lot of alcohol and smoked a lot of tobacco.

Everything was made to "lighten our load." Our dishes and appliances were colorful turquoise, pink, orange, yellow, red, lavender, everything imaginable. A lot of designs were influenced by the atomic age imagery motifs. Cars grew fins. Ashtrays and coffee tables took on the shape of flying wedges. Our vacuum cleaners were shaped like the Sputnik. The market was flooded with loads of inexpensive plastic and aluminum. It was the beginning of T.V. dinners, fast food and "portable" everything. We had steam irons with 15 vents instead of 4. This was probably one of the most scary and wonderfully inventive periods in history.

Visiting the antique shops you will see many 50s and 60s kitchen items. For those who are used to much older "antiques, it's hard to believe these items would be collectible, and for those who lived through the period it is difficult to believe that they are still useable. But, the wonderful bright, airy colors for dishes, appliances and furniture still appeal to the eye and give a sense of the excitement of the era.

Who collects these items? Well, today there are more and more people. The 50s and 60s are back in Vogue. The checkered floors, floral curtains, chrome toasters, red appliances, aqua tables and chairs, are being collected and used. Their fun, warm, daring motifs and feeling make them a favorite of today's decorators.

Part of the reason for the popularity of the era is the warm sense of nostalgia it conjures up in us. In the advertising and television shows of the time, the house wife was portrayed as a smiling, happy, lady singing while cleaning the kitchen floor, wearing a shirtwaist dress. The mop was sponge and the floor black and white checks. Spic and Span was her cleaner. Everything was push button, televisions, ovens, mixers. The infinite varieties of color and shape that plastic enabled showed up in utensils, gadgets and dishes were plastic.

The western look was at the height of popularity. Cowboys like Roy Rogers, Tom Mix, Hopalong Cassidy, and Gene Autry were all T.V. heros. Cowboy dishes, furniture and clothing became a popular fad among children and adults alike.

The memories of this era continue to charm us: the drive-in fast food places and the drive-in movies; the jazzed up Chevy's and convertibles; the soda fountains with real ice cream sodas. The memories are of a simpler, happy, fun time. And it's all coming back!

Whether you are collecting the 50s-60s kitchen items to use or to display, they can be a good investment. But do go slow! Buy what you like and what you can put to good use. Mix up your colors and get the real feel of the era.

Collecting the 50s and 60s Kitchen : A Handbook and Price Guide will help you identify your collectibles and will be valuable in pricing your items. The prices reflect the markets in the mid-west and may differ slightly from those in other regions. They also reflect items in the condition shown. As condition and availability vary, so do the prices. Nevertheless, this book will give the collector-decorator a good idea of what an item is worth on the market today. (Please note auction prices may differ from shop prices.)

I hope you use and enjoy this book as much as I enjoyed creating it, and I wish you all happy collecting.

Ceramic busts of mammy and chef with mouths open. Japan. 2 7/8". $60-70.

Five piece kitchen set. $25-30.

Plastic juice reamer with seed filter. $18-22.

Plastic juicer from Lusterware. $5-6.

Plastic juicer made in U.S.A. $3-4.

Plastic bar set. Corkscrew, opener, mixers. $17-23.

King Tappers plastic bottle caps. $7-10.

Plastic kitchen utensils. 11". $3-4 each.

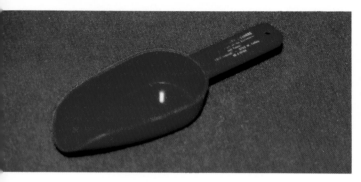

Plastic ladle. 13". $5-7.

Plastic scoop with advertising on it. 6". $4-6.

Salad tongs. $4-6.

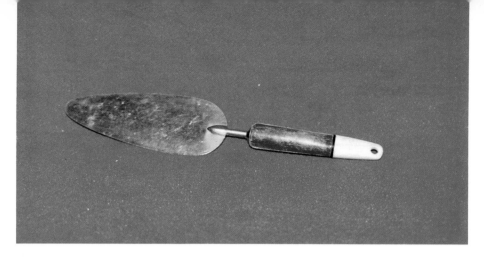

Metal cake server with wood handle. 11". $3-4.

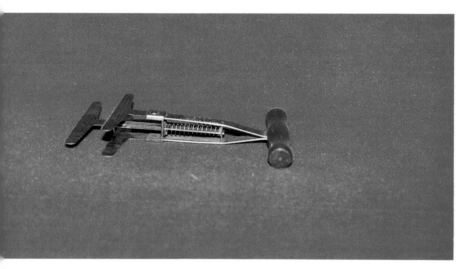

Metal chopper with wood handle. 8". $5-7.

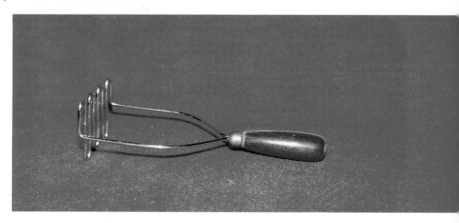

Metal masher with wood handle. 10". $4-6.

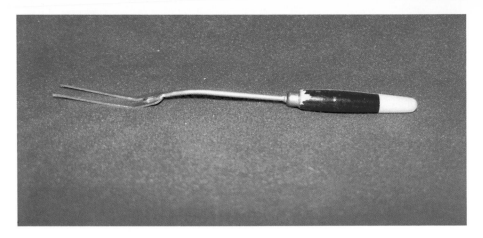

Metal meat fork with wood handle. 13 1/2". $2-4.

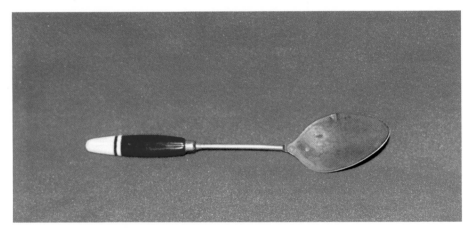

Metal spoon with wood handle. 12". $2-4.

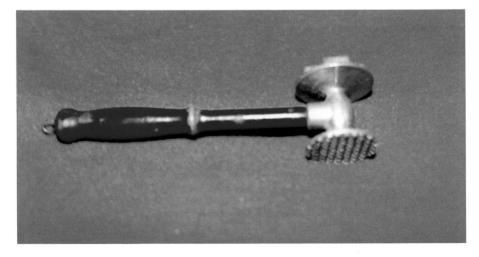

Metal meat tenderizer. $10-15.

Wooden meat tenderizer. $8-12.

Plastic cookie cutter by Bisquick, Bonny
Ware. $5-8.

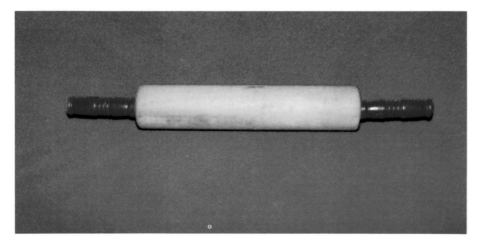

Wooden rolling pin. 15". $10-15.

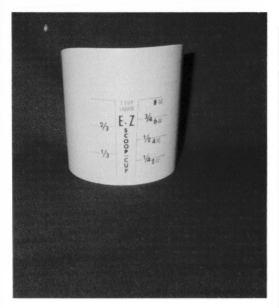

E-Z Scoop measuring cup with advertising on bottom. $4-7.

Plastic measuring jar by Rogers Products. 8". $4-6.

Mustard dispenser by Tappit. Bakelite holder, glass jar. 5". $15-20,

Shaker by Stanley Home Products. $8-12.

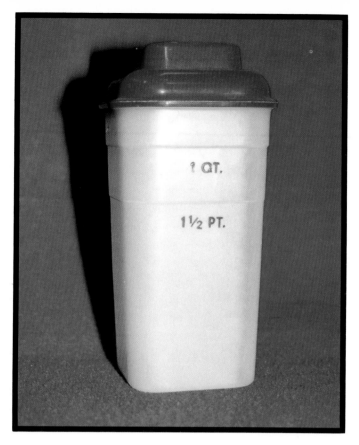

Plastic shaker and measure bottle. 8 1/2". $6-8.

Canned milk holder by the Carnation Co. The
lid punches a hole in can. $15-20.

Cookie King cookie press made from copper.
$30-35.

Flour sifter from Bromwell's Super Fine
Flour. $10-15.

Satin glass measure and shaker from C.S. Co.
13". $20-30.

Plastic tape dispenser. $4-6.

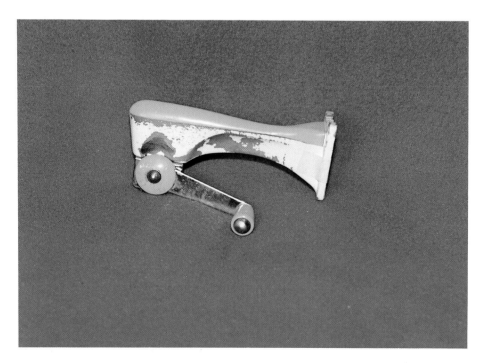

Metal can opener by Vaughn, U.S.A. $8-12.

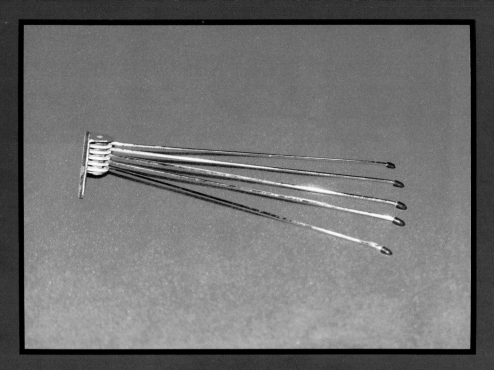

Stainless steel tea towel holder by
Swing-away. $10-15.

Waste Bag Holder by Bag-It-All. "Home
metal products." $15-20.

Table Accessories and Dishes

Melmac service for four dinnerware set. $20-30.

Melmac set of dishes by Royalon, Inc. Service
for 6. 1950s. $45-55.

Melmac set of dishes by Royalon, Inc. Service
for 4. 1950s. $25-35.

Gold tone dishes, setting for four. $40-50.

Ceramic coffee set by Kaysons International,
1966. $16-22.

"Fiesta" dinner plate. 7 1/2". Grey. $12-15.

"Fiesta" dinner plate. 10". Pink. $25-30.

"Fiesta" bowl, 8 1/2". Forest green. $22-25.

"Tamac" Pottery ashtray. $12-14.

"Fiesta" bowl, 8 1/2". Chartreuse. $40-45.

"Tamac" Pottery cup and saucer. $18-22.

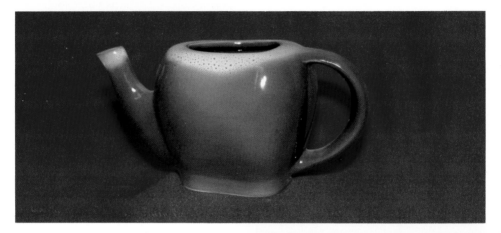

"Tamac" Pottery tea pot. $25-28.

"Tamac" Pottery bowl. $10-12.

"Tamac" Pottery, Perry, Oklahoma. Cream and sugar, salt and pepper. $30-35 set.

"Tamac" Pottery place setting. $40-45.

"Tamac" Pottery vase. $22-25.

"Tamac" Pottery divided vegetable dish. $12-15.

Insulated plastic cup, bowl, glasses. $5-7
each.

Set of 4 insulated coffee mugs by NFC
Thermal. $10-15 set.

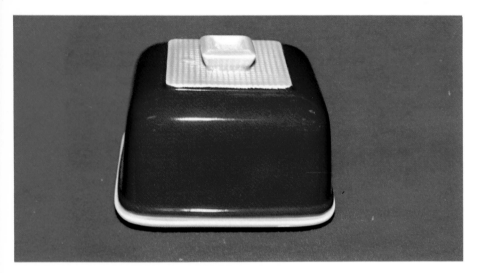

Ceramic toast holder. 5 1/2" x 4". $18-22.

Refrigerator divided jam and jelly dish. 5 1/2" x 2 1/2". $10-14.

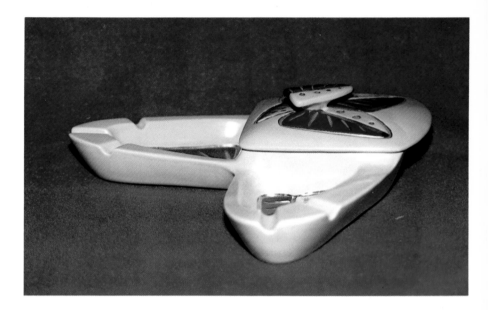

Ceramic covered ashtray by Williams. 12 1/2". $20-25.

Ceramic platter by designer Sascha Brastoff. 15 1/2" square. $60-75.

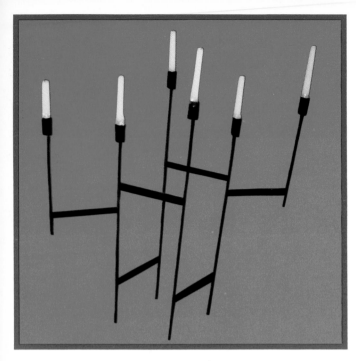

Wrought iron candle holder. 31". $100-125.

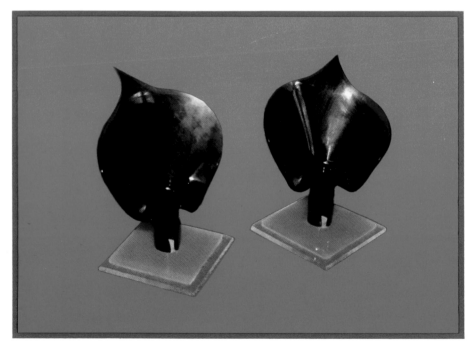

Lucite candle holders. 10". $40-50.

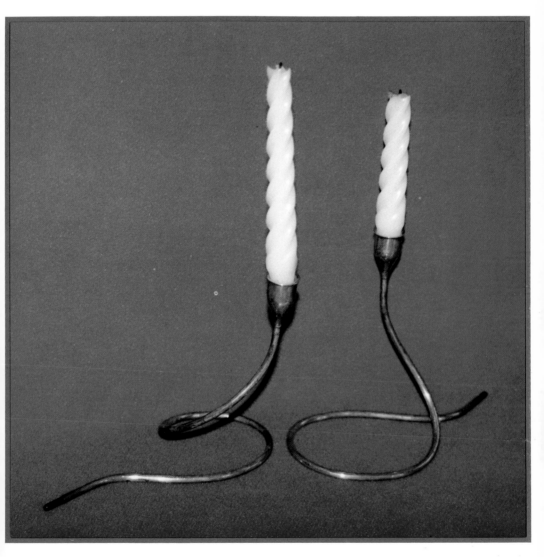

Sterling silver candle holders. 16". $200-240.

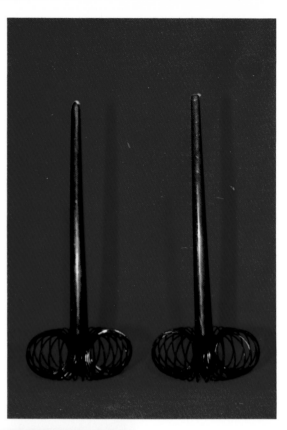

Wire candle holders. $20-28 set.

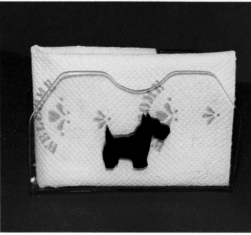

Clear plastic napkin holder with Scottie dog on front. $8-12.

Wall-hung plastic napkin holder. $22-27.

Brass and wrought iron paper bag holder. 10" x 11". $10-15.

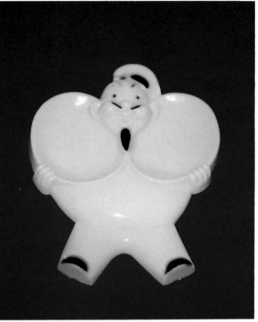

Plastic spoon rest, made in Japan. $5-8.

Chef plastic napkin holder. $8-12.

Anodized aluminum butter dish. $5-7.

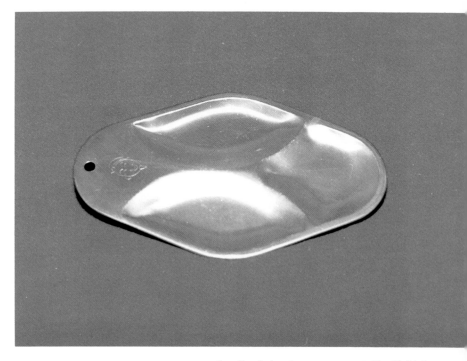

Anodized aluminum spoon rest. 8" x 5". $4-6.

Cream and sugar set from F & F, Dayton, Ohio. $12.50-15.

Cream and sugar set by Federal Tool Corporation. $150-$200.

Milk, Syrup and Water Pitchers

Plastic pitcher and four cups with handles.
$20-25.

Plastic water pitcher. $12-15.

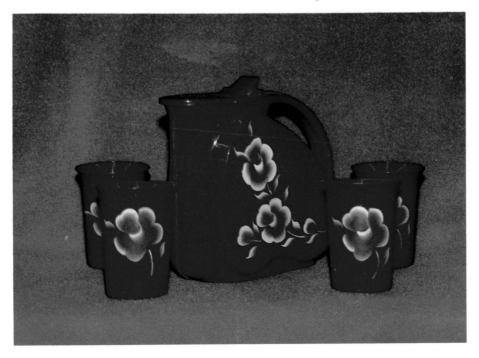

Plastic pitcher with glasses by Titan. Floral
patterns on fronts. $10-15.

Anodized aluminum pitcher with plastic
handle. "Color Craft". 8". $12-15.

Anodized aluminum pitcher. 7 3/4". "Norben
ware". $28-30.

Anodized aluminum pitcher. 7 3/4".
"Flamingo by Nasco". $14-18.

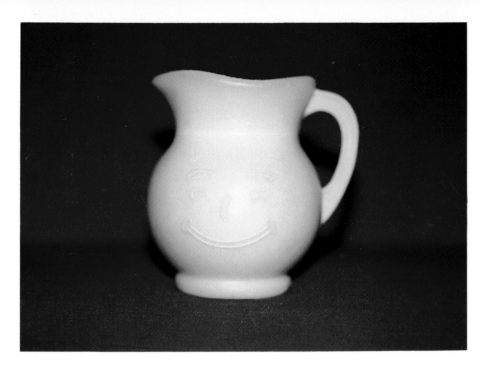

Kool-aid plastic pitcher. $10-15.

Insulated plastic water/juice pitcher. $10-15.   Plastic water pitcher. $14-18.

Red Wing ceramic water pitcher with a quail of front. 12". $25-30.

Red Wing ceramic water pitcher with a table on the front. 12". $15-20.

Douglass glass fondue set. 8". $6.50-10.

Douglass glass coffee pot. 6 1/2". $6.50-10.   Douglass glass coffee pot. 7 1/4". $7.50-12.

Douglass glass canister jar. 7 3/4". $5.50-9.

Glass syrup jar with plastic lid. $4-8.

Douglass glass batter jar. 9". $4.50-9.

Pair of syrup jars with plastic caps. Hand
painted scene. 6", $15-18. 10", $22-25.

Glass syrup jar with plastic handle. $20-25.

Glass syrup jar with plastic handle. $8-10.

Glass syrup pitcher with plastic handle. $5-8.

Candy, Vegetable and Fruit Bowls

Candy dish. Silver plate on enamel. "Reed and Barton." $35-40.

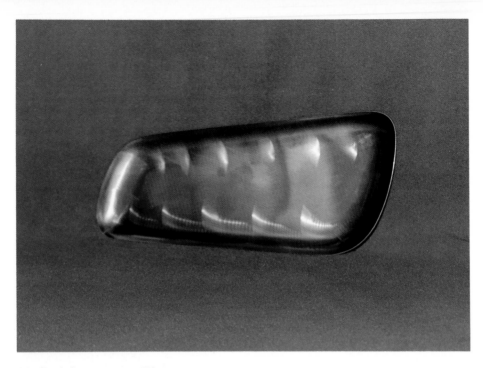

Anodized aluminum tray. "Eloxsoren,
Norway." 18" x 8". $20-25.

Candy dish. Silver plate on enamel. "Reed
and Barton." $35-40.

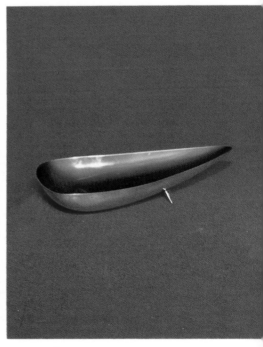

Footed candy dish. Silver plate on enamel.
"Reed and Barton." $40-45.

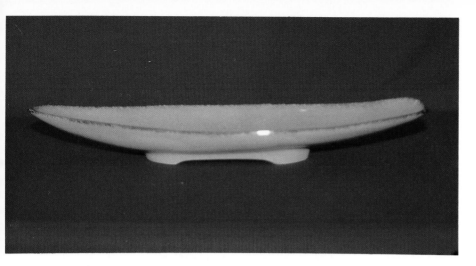

Ceramic candy dish by Calif. originals. 20".
$15-18.

Plastic sectioned candy/relish dish on metal
stand. $8-12.

Handcrafted divided china relish tray.
Winfield China from California. 16 1/2". $18-
25.

Sectioned ceramic candy/ relish dish with
metal handle. $12-15.

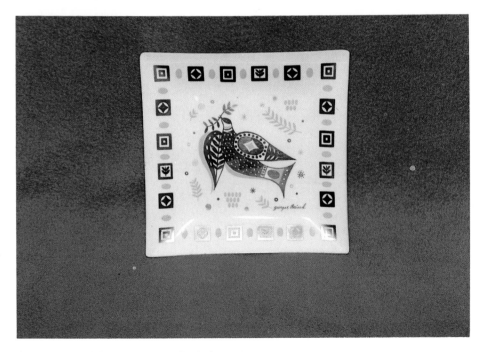

Glass candy dish by Georges Briard. 8". $30-40.

Candy dish china with gold inlay flowers. 6".
"Imari Mauri." $30-40.

Glass fruit bowl on metal stand. 10" x 6". $12-16.

Venetian glass ash tray. 6" x 2". $50-60.

Set of Red Wing casseroles with candle
warmer and wrought iron holder. Two quart.
$95-120.

Ceramic pear shape chip and dip bowl. 10" x 13". $16-21.

Roseville tray #95-10. 7 1/2" x 11". $45-60.

 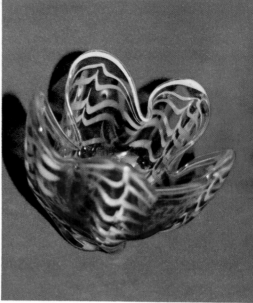

Venetian glass candy dish. 6 1/2". $80-100.   Venetian glass bowl, 7". $90-110.

Lucite salad bowl with fork and spoon. 10".
$20-28.

Plastic revolving candy dish in brass holder.
$12-15.

Front: Resin fruit dish. $15-20; rear: candy
server. $15-20. Beaded fruit 7 pieces. $20-25.

Three tier club aluminum server. 11". $17-22.

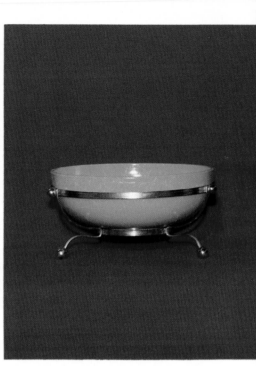

Glass bowl in brass footed stand. 10". $12-15.

Pottery lazy Susan by Valley Vista Pottery of California. $55-65.

Ceramic lazy Susan snack set made in
California. 18". $15-18.

Lucite snack caddy with brass stand. 12". $10-15.

Three tier party tray. "Ebonette by Knowles."
$25-35.

Plastic server with sugar, creamer, and four
coasters. Federal Tool Co. $15-20.

Aluminum party tray-lazy Susan. 21". $24-30.

Candy dish by Ideal California. Matte finish.
$10-15.

Candy dish by California Originals. 8". $8-10.

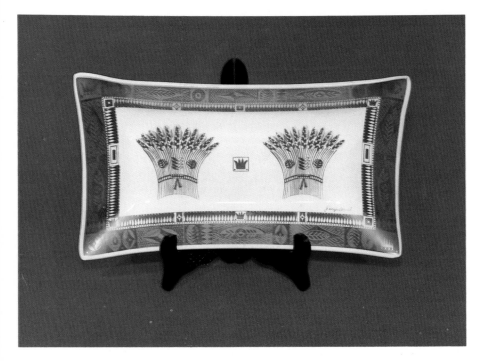

Glass bread tray by designer, George Briard.
7" x 11 1/2" White with gold trim. $35-40.

Clear glass candy bowl. 6". $9-12.

Anodized aluminum refrigerator container.
$8-10.

Forks and plastic salad bowl. $8-12.

Set of four glass bowls. $35-45.

Anodized aluminum dish. $12-18.

Canisters, Bread and Cake Keepers

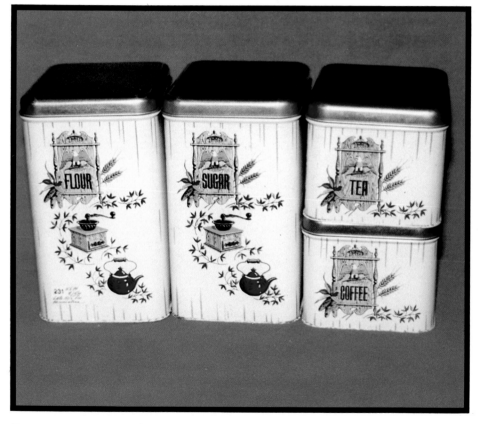

Four piece tin canister set. $20-25.

Four piece busy baker tin canister set. $25-35.

Four piece metal canister set with step on
trash can. $25-38.

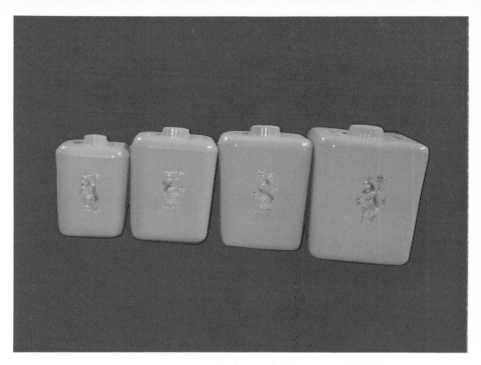

Canister set by Lusterware. $28-35.

Canister set of plastic. $15-20. Missing a
canister.

Copper canister set with salt and pepper set
by Westbend. $35-45.

Tin canister set with painted on sail boats.
$35-45.

Metal enamel cake carrier. 12" x 8". $20-25.

Metal and copper cake keeper. 12" square.
$15-19.

Cake keeper clear plastic cover. $15-22.

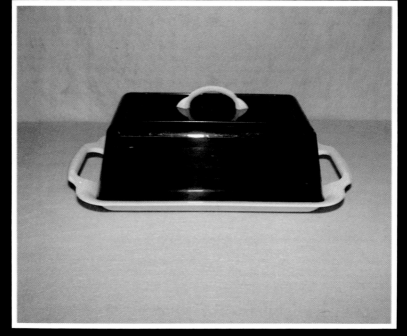

Plastic cake keeper. $18-25.

Copper cake holder by Westbend. $15-20.

Plastic bread keeper by Burroughs Corporation. $18-24.

Bread board and keeper with metal top and wood bottom. 12" x 12". $20-32.

Bread keeper from Burroughs. $15-20.

Plastic bread keeper marked U.S.A. $25-35.

Bread box by Lusterware. $25-30.

Plastic bread box. $28-35.

Bread box by Lusterware. $25-35.

Salt and Pepper Sets

Five piece ceramic spice set with mammy
and chefs embossed on the front. $125-150
set.

Ceramic chef and mammy holding fruit salt
and pepper set. 3 1/2". $40-50.

Aunt Jemima and Uncle Mose salt and
pepper set, from F & F, Dayton, Ohio. Large
set. $65-75.

Ceramic cook and chef salt and pepper set.
3". $35-40.

Mammy and chef ceramic salt and pepper set
from Japan. 4 1/2". $45-50.

Mammy and chef ceramic busts salt and
pepper set. 3". $45-55.

Large head boy ceramic salt and pepper set
from Japan. 3 1/2". $40-50.

Ceramic mammy and chef salt and pepper
set. 5". $50-60.

Ceramic mammy and chef salt and pepper
set from Japan. 5". $40-50.

Young mammy and chef salt and pepper set.
3". $35-45.

Ceramic dog and cat salt and pepper set. 3".
$15-20.

Stainless steel Scottie dog pulling wagon
with salt and pepper set. $25-35.

Rose ceramic salt and pepper set on a leaf
tray. 5" x 3". $12-15.

Sprinkling can salt and pepper set. $6-9.

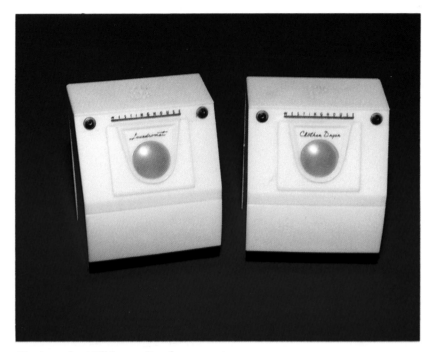

Plastic washer and dryer salt and pepper set
by Westinghouse. $25-30.

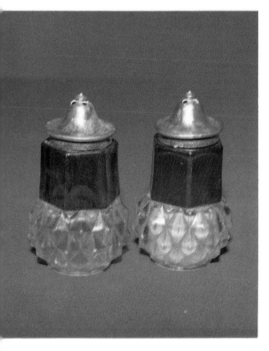

Lucite salt and pepper set. $4-7.

Bakelite salt and pepper set. $12-15.

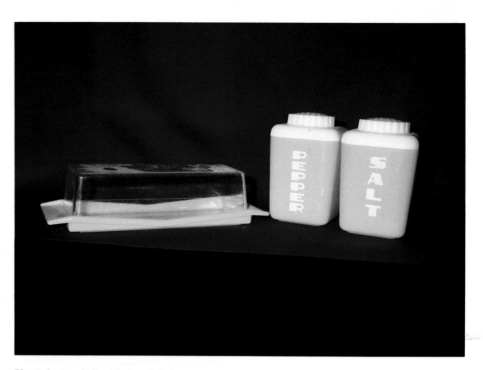

Plastic butter dish with clear lid. $5-7. Salt & Pepper set. $5-7.

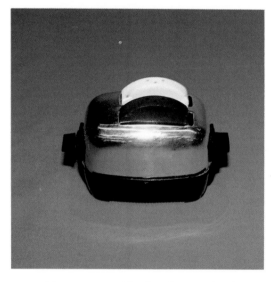

Plastic toaster with salt and pepper toast. $14-18.

Plastic ship salt and pepper set. $6-9.

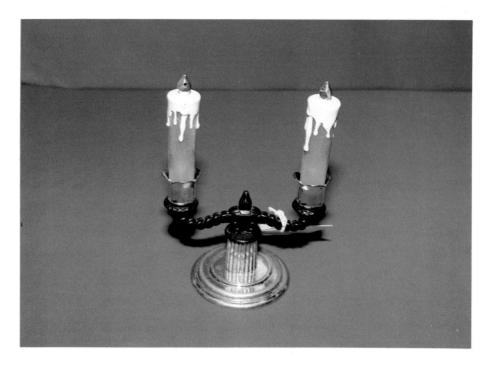

Plastic candelabra salt and pepper set. $9-12.

Plastic salt and pepper set by Trump plastics. 3 1/2". $10-14.

Salt and pepper set with chef on front of tray. $15-20.

Plastic salt and pepper set. 3 1/2". $5-8.

Clear glass salt and pepper set. 3". $6-8.

Red ceramic salt and pepper set. 2 1/2" x 3 1/2". $14-18.

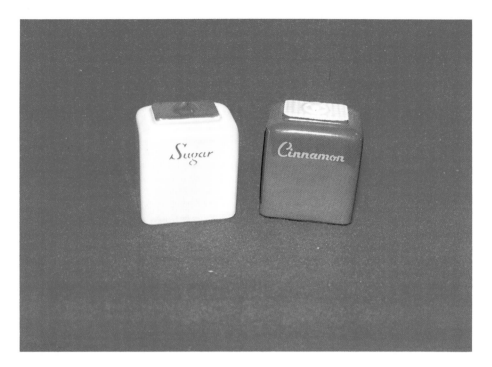

Sugar and cinnamon shakers. 2" x 3". $8-10.

Wood salt and pepper set. 4 1/2". $5-9.

Ceramic cactus salt and pepper set. 3 1/2". $12-15.

Cats salt and pepper set, U.S.A. $8-12.

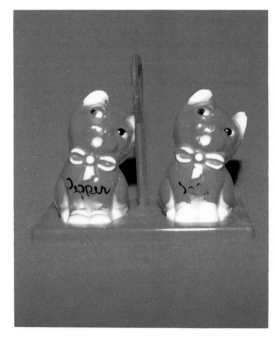

Plastic kittens salt and pepper set in holder.
3". $12-15.

Salt and pepper plastic set, U.S.A. $4-6.

Cat and dog salt and pepper set from F & F,
Dayton.
Ohio. $12-16.

Cows salt and pepper set of plastic by J.D.'s
of N.Y. $8-12.

Plastic mallets salt and pepper set. $7-12.

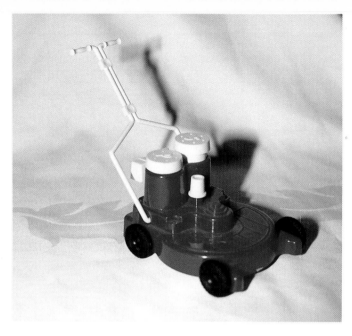

Plastic salt and pepper set as a lawn mower.
$20-25.

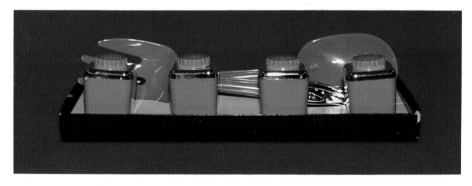

Plastic salad set in box by Sterlite products.
$8-10.

Anodized aluminum spoon rest & salt and
pepper set. $6-8.

Textiles

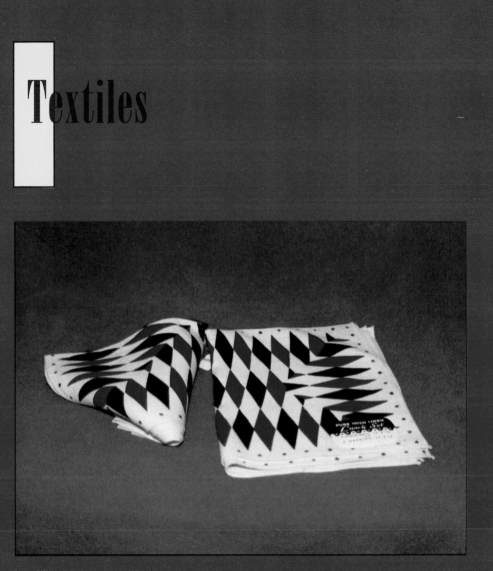

Set of four placemats and four napkins made of Irish linen. $18-23.

Belgian linen tea towel with cat on front. 16" x 30". $15-25.

Belgian linen tea towel with kittens imprinted on material, by Tammis Keefe. 16" x 30". $15-22.

Floral cotton tablecloth. $22-25.

Grapes and vine cotton tablecloth. $35-40.

Red floral cotton tablecloth. $35-45.

Colorful fruit cotton tablecloth. $15-20.

Mexican scene cotton tablecloth. $35-45.

Mexican dancers cotton tablecloth. $30-40.

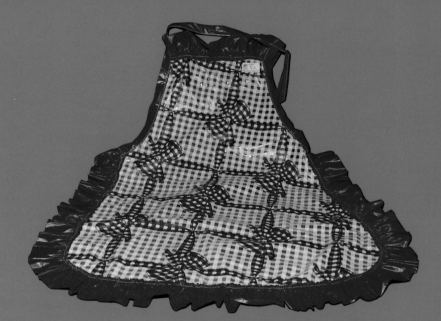

Plastic apron with bow print. $6-8.

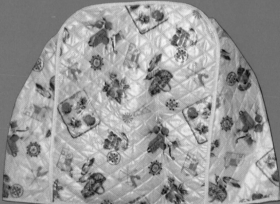

Plastic quilted toaster cover. 16". $7-10.

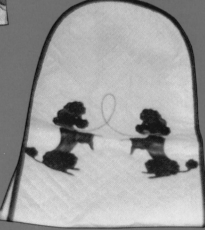

Quilted plastic blender cover. 14". $8-12.

Plastic lace place mats. 7". $4-6.

Crochet bloomers hot pads. $2-3.

Crochet pansy hot pad. $3-4.

Needlepoint pot holder. $3-4.

Crochet pot holder. $1-2.

Cotton face hot pad. $2-3.

Glasses and Bar Items

Wildflower thermal ice bucket. 10". $20-30.

Wildflower thermal glasses with rack. $35-40.

Anodized aluminum shot glasses. 2 1/4".
$38-40 set.

Set of six Colorado centennial frosted glasses.
1959. $60-75.

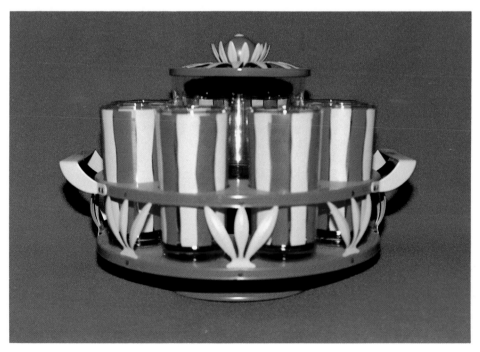

6 glasses with lazy Susan holder. $35-40.

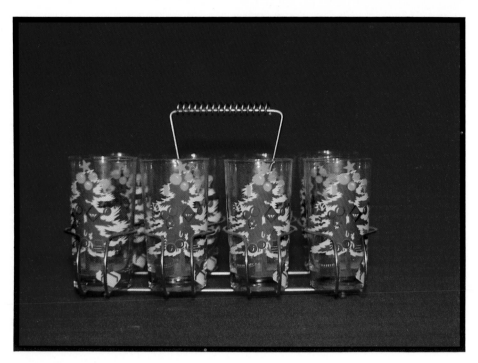

Set of eight Christmas glasses in wire holder.
$35-45.

Metal and plastic, glass holders.
"Coasterettes". Set of four. $20-25.

Set of 4 designer 12 ounce glasses with gold
trim. "Georges Briard". $35-40. set.

Set of eight glasses in brass holder. 16 ounces,
gold trim. $25-35.

Yellow glasses and pitcher in wire rack. $40-50.

Aluminum 8 ounce tumbler. $10-12 each.

Set of 6 frosted glasses, leather bound with western motif. $18-22.

Hostess glass holder with wood rack. $32-38.

Four 6 ounce glasses by Libby Glass
Company with painted instruments on each
glass. $14-18.

Set of eight glasses by the designer Pasinski.
$30-35.

Set of six cordial glasses with wrought iron holder. $18-25.

Bar set, chrome spritzer and six glasses. "Soda King". $110-135.

Crooked glasses and shaker. $20-28.

Glass, with silver overlay, cocktail set. $40-50.

Ice crusher. Plastic bottom with metal crusher. $12-16.

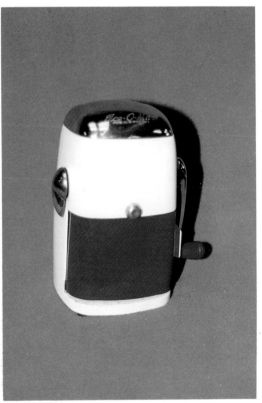

Ice crusher by Ice-O-Matic. $30-40.

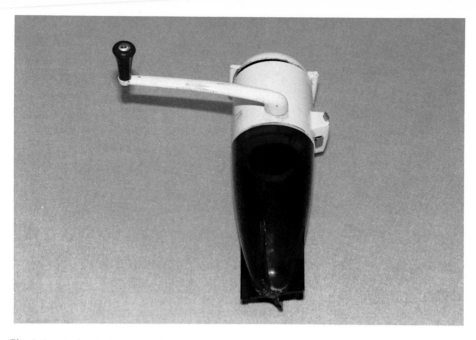

Plastic ice crusher by Dazey, St. Louis,
Missouri. $20-25.

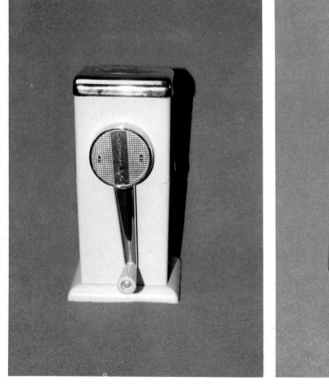

Ice crusher by Ice-O-Matic. $25-35.

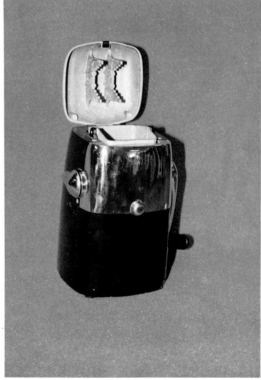

Ice crusher by Ice-O-Matic. $30-40.

Plastic spice grater by Lilo, Italy. $35-40.

Plastic coated ice bucket. $15-20.

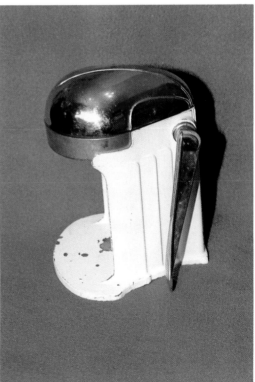

Juice-O-Mat By Rival Mfg. Co. Pot metal. 9" x 6". $15-20.

Aluminum ice bucket with plastic handles.
$12-15.

Aluminum ice bucket with Bakelite handles.
$15-20.

Bar shaker with glass bottom and chrome top. 10". $20-25.

Plastic novelty bottle for booze. 7". $10-15.

Glass drink mixer. 7". $9-12.

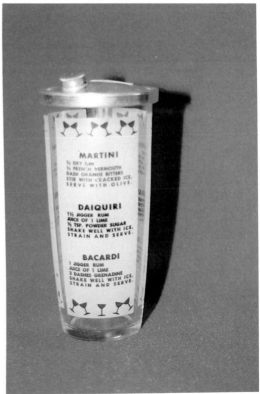

Bar shaker with glass jar and metal lid. 8". $15-20.

Coaster and nut plastic set. $12-15.

Hazel Atlas four piece cocktail set. Amethyst
Moroccan. $45-60.

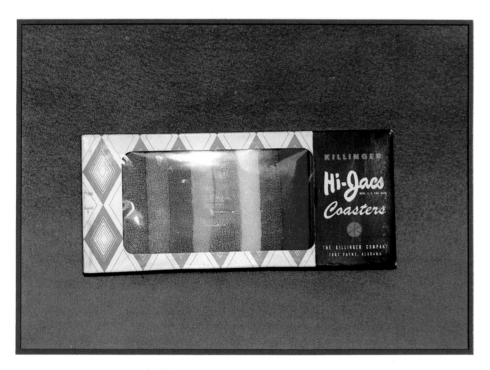

Hi-Jacs terry cloth coasters. $9-12.

Set of Lucite coasters in holder. 4" x 4 1/2".
$16-22.

Three piece bar set with black musicians as
implements. $35-45.

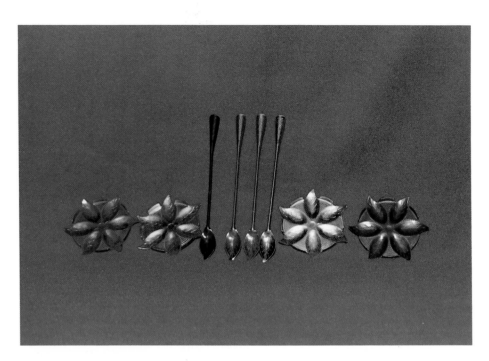

Anodized aluminum spoons and spoon rests.
$30-35 set.

Set of 4 lucite snack trays and glass holders
by Alexander and Wilson Co. $18-25.

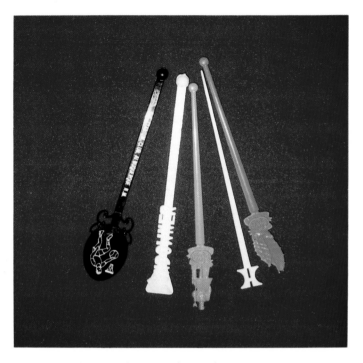

Figural plastic drink stirrers. $2-3 each.

Anodized aluminum coasters. 3 1/4". $18-20.

Tin beer tray, advertising Schlitz beer. 13".
1968. $20-25.

Tin beer tray, advertising Schlitz beer. 13".
1957. $25-30.

Tin beer tray, advertising Budweiser beer.
13". 1968. $30-35.

Tin beer tray, advertising Miller beer. 13".
1955. $15-20.

Clocks and Appliances

Eight-day wind up sunburst clock. Wood and
brass. "Germany". $100-140.

Copper and brass kitchen clock by West
Clock Co. 7". $8-12.

Plastic Spartus kitchen clock. 8". $18-25.

Enameled metal Gilbert kitchen clock. 7 1/2".
$30-35.

Catalin clock by Telechron. $50-65.

General Electric kitchen clock. $20-25.

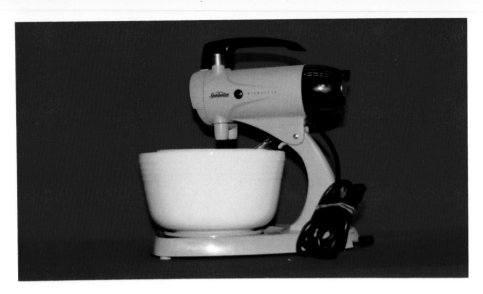

Sunbeam Mix Master twelve-speed mixer
with two bowls. $55-75.

Metal hanging lights. $225-250.

Plastic electric butter keeper. $35-45.

Sunbeam electric chrome two quart tea kettle.
$25-35.

Electric coffee pot. $35-45.

Oster two-speed blender with glass jar. $40-50.

Waffle iron with Bakelite handles and chrome temperature gauge. $25-35.

Chrome coffee server with Bakelite handle. $8-12.

Sunbeam chrome coffee pitcher. 9". $20-30.

Cory chrome coffee pot with Bakelite handle.
$40-50.

G.E. chrome two slice toaster. $12-18.

Toastmaster one slice chrome toaster. $30-40.

Planters, Wall Pockets and Wall Hangers

Wire cart holding ceramic planter. 7" x 3 1/2". $6-9.

Plastic planter with man on bike in silhouette. 9" x 12". $14-18.

Ceramic planter 4" x 4 1/2". $8-12.

Ceramic planter with brass fixture by California Pottery Co. $9-14.

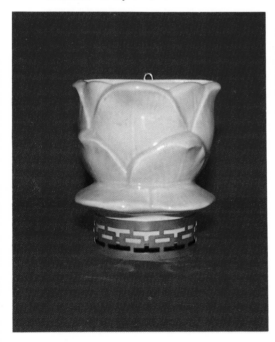

Wall pocket by Plastic Products, Hollywood, California. $12-16.

Ceramic wall pocket by Maddux of California. 5". $10-14.

Ceramic daisy wall pocket. 8". $20-25.

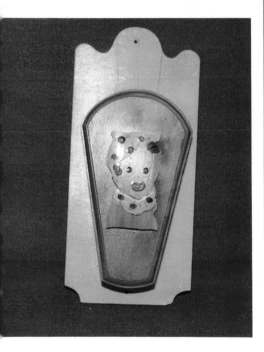

Wooden mammy note holder. $60-75.

Wooden wall knife holder with mammy on the front. $55-65.

Wooden mammy memo holder. $50-60.

Wooden little girl grocery list. $65-75.

Wooden folk art mammy note holder. $45-55.

Rare tin mammy egg timer and pot holder.
8". $125-150.

Cook Books

Housewife's Handbook by Wm. H. Wise Co., Inc., 1952. $15-20.

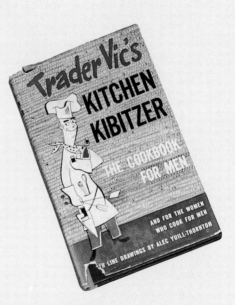

Trader Vic's Cookbook for Men by Doubleday. 1952 $8-12.

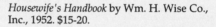

The Good Cook's Encyclopedia by Pamela Fry, 1962. $10-15.

Foodarama Party Book. E.P. Dutton & Co. 1959.
$3-5.

Saucepans and the Single Girl by Jinx Kragen
and Judy Perry, 1955. $15-20.

Better Homes and Gardens New Cook Book. 1953.
$10-15.

The Seventeen Cookbook. MacMillan Co. 1964.
$6-10.

Cook Book for Two. Garden City books. 1957.
$5-8.

The Art of Salad Making. Doubleday & Co.
1968. $5-8.

365 Ways to Cook Hamburger. Doubleday &
Co. 1958. $5-8.

A Salute to Chocolate. Gramercy books. 1968.
$8-11.

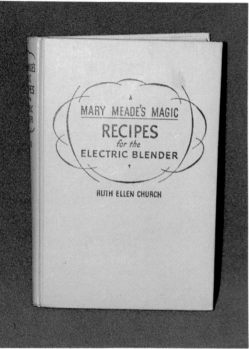

Mary Mead's Magic Recipes for the Electric *Blender*. The Bobbs-Merrill Co. 1956. $4-7.

The Betty Furness Westinghouse Cook Book. Simon & Schuster. 1954. $15-20.

Lessons in Gourmet Cooking. Hearthside Press Co. 1963. $7-12.

The No Cooking Cookbook. Coward-McCann. 1962. $4-7.

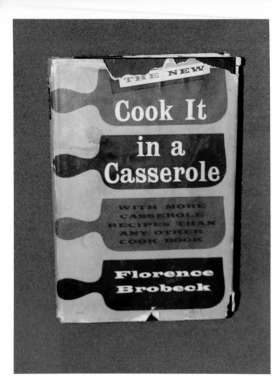

Cook It in a Casserole. M. Burrows & Co. 1955. $5-8.

Cutco Cook Book. Cutco Division. 1961 $6-9.

The Pillsbury Family Cookbook. The Pillsbury Co. 1960. $10-15.

Standard Oster Blender Recipe Book. 1957. $10-12.

Furniture

Limed oak china hutch, 38" x 60". $325-375.

Glass table with aluminum base. Four wood
pretzel chairs by George Mulhouser. $800-900
per chair; table, $450-550.

Table, five chairs and buffet. Heavy lacquer,
bleached mahogany by designer, Paul
McCobb. The Calvin Group, Grand Rapids,
Michigan. $1500-1,800.

Five-piece formica kitchen set. $275-300.

Formica table and chair set with self storing
leaf. $350-450.

Wrought iron tea cart with formica top and
plastic wheels. $85-100.

Chrome table and chairs. $300-350.

Child's formica and chrome table and chairs.
$140-190.

Formica and chrome kitchen set. $350-425.

Thornet Originals, restaurant chairs. Wood
with upholstered seats. $100-140 each.

Vinyl-coated metal game chairs with leather
seats and backs. Designer, Charles Eames.
$325-375. each.

Kitchen set, cabinet, table and chairs. $600-700.

Formica table and chair set. $340-410.

Western Items

Child's cowboy and Indian motif cups by
Hazel Atlas Glass Co. 6 ounce. $12-15 each.

Western glass mug set with wooden carrier.
$50-60.

Bar stool, vinyl and pine. Seat lifts up. 42".
$200-250 set of 4.

Six frosted 16 ounce tumblers in wooden
holder. $15-20.

Western Monterey platter. 16" x 9 3/4". $65-75.

Western Monterey plate. 10". $20-24.

Western Monterey enamel coffee pot. $125-150.

Western enamel plate, made in Mexico. 10".
$15-20.

Western enamel coffee mug, made in Mexico.
$15-20.

Cowboy enamel steak plate with wooden
tray. $25-30.

Western wooden snack set with trays. $90-
120.

Cowboy enamel bowl. 6 1/2". $18-25.

Western Del Coronado, ceramic salad bowl.
11". $90-120.

Del Coronado ceramic mug set. $40-50.

Del Coronado ceramic cream and sugar. $60-75

Tin Davy Crockett trash can. 9 1/2". $40-50.

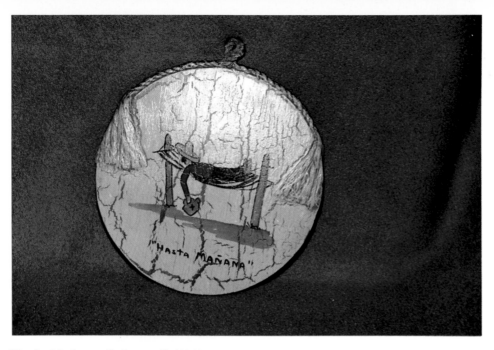

Wooden Mexican wall placque. 8". $18-22.

Wallace China restaurant coffee mug. $30-35.

Horseshoe chrome fireplace set. 16". $60-80.

Wooden tray, made in Mexico. 8" x 17". $20-25.

Wooden Mexican coaster holder. $8-10.

Wooden nut bowl with mallet made in Mexico. 9 3/4". $25-29.

Miscellaneous

Ceramic mammy clothes sprinkler. 8". $175-
225.

Coffee warmer, copper, wrought iron holder
with wooden feet. 14" x 16". $120-145.

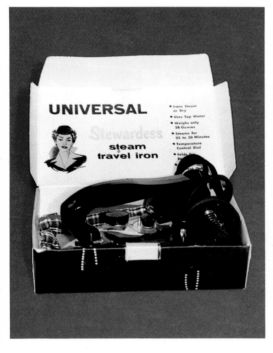

Travel steam iron by Universal. Bakelite
handle. $40-50.

Plastic laundry sprinkler. 7". $7-10.

Enamel double boiler cooking pan. $14-18.

Bread basket, U.S.A. $6-8.

Ceramic tile trivet. 6". $6-9.

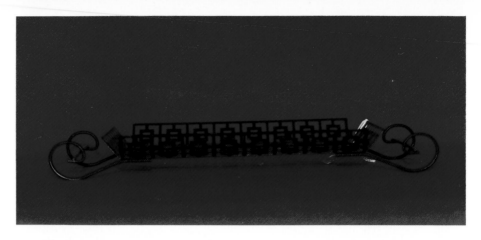

Wrought iron cracker tray. 15" x 6". $5-8.

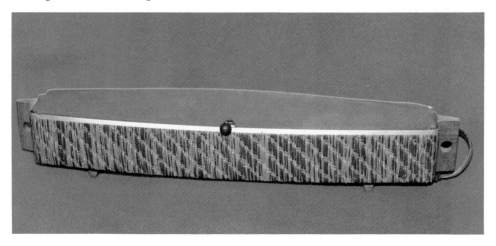

Wire glass holder. Holds 8 glasses. $10-15.

Automatic electric bread warmer. Salton Inc.
23 1/2" x 5 1/2". $15-20.

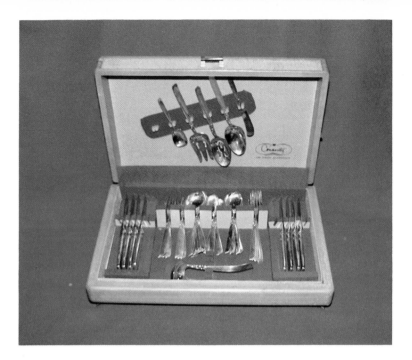

Community "South Seas" silver plate set for 8 dinnerware in original blonde oak case. $150-175.

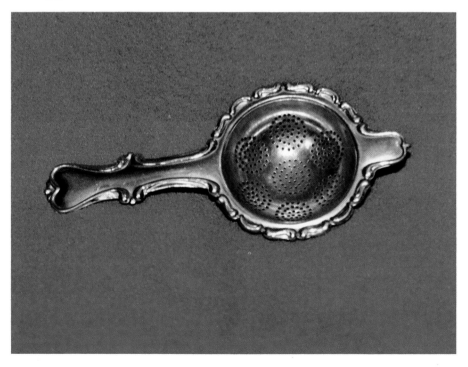

Tea strainer by Alfra, Italy. 7" x 3". 15-20.

Chrome wax paper/paper towels/foil wrap
holder. $15-20.

Caloric wax paper/paper towels/foil holder.
$25-35.

Ceramic rooster wall pocket. 9". $22-28.

Set of six metal trays. (4 small trays, 1
medium, 1 large) $30-40.

Painted metal serving tray. 18". $5-7.

Match holder made of plastic. $6-10.

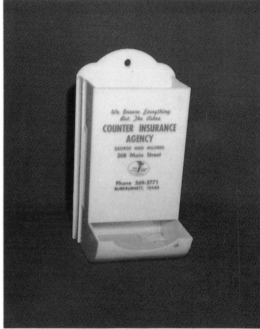

Match holder advertising Counter Ins. Co. $8-14.

Large plastic refrigerator jar. Wire closure. $8-10.

Small plastic refrigerator jar. Wire closure. $4-6.

Office waste can with plastic and imitation leather covering. 13". 12-15.

Kitchen metal waste basket. 14 1/2". $8-10.

Metal waste basket. 11 1/2". $6-8.

Tin plaid recipe box. $4-6.

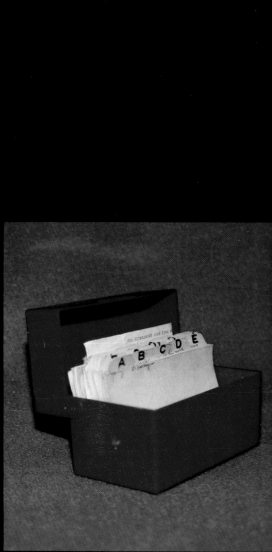

Plastic recipe box by Fosta Products. $15-20.

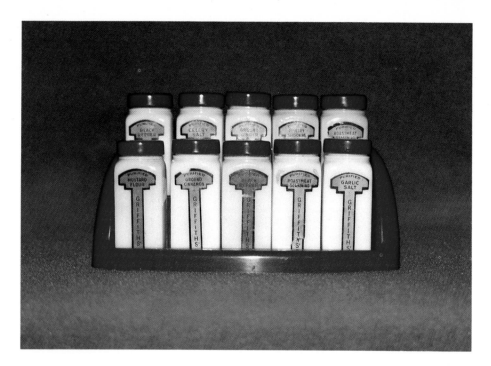

Griffith eight-piece glass spice set made in
U.S.A. $30-40.

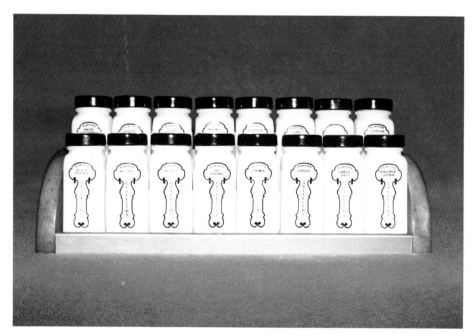

Griffith sixteen-piece glass spice set made in
U.S.A. $50-60.

Griffith twelve-piece glass spice set made in
U.S.A. $40-50.

Plastic covered character bowl. $5-7.

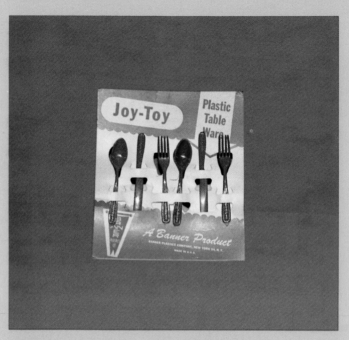

Child's tableware by Joy Toy, Banner, New
York. $8-12.

Child's Lusterware china tea set. "Japan". $85-
100.

Child's plastic Campbell Soup cup. $9-12.

Picnic set in original box. Tin holders with plastic dishes. $75-90.

Cookie Jars

Laughing mammy cookie jar with lid in her
belly by Rockingham Pottery. 8 1/2". $300-
350.

Aunt Jemima plastic cookie jar by F & F,
Dayton, Ohio. $375-450.

Ceramic mammy cookie jar from McCoy
Pottery. 10 1/2". $185-225.

Plastic Santa cookie jar by Empire U.S.A. $40-
50.

Plastic Aladdin Paddy's Pig cookie jar. $35-
45.